in isolation
an anthology

alternative field notes

ISBN: 978-1-7361296-0-9
1st Print, December 4, 2020
2nd Print, February 2021

Book layout and design by Jessica Ceballos y Campbell for Alternative Field Notes. A special thank you to Karineh Mahdessian and Angelina Sáenz for helping sort through the massive amount of submissions we received.

www.alternativefield.com | www.avenue50studio.org

In early 2020, we invited poets to submit poetry inspired by and related to their experiences at the onset of the pandemic and its resulting quarantine.

Because COVID-19 is a contagious virus and to further combat its ability to overwhelm our healthcare system, Los Ángeles Mayor Eric Garcetti issued a "Safer at Home" emergency order - instructing all residents of the City of Los Angeles to stay inside and immediately limit all movement outside of our homes beyond what is absolutely necessary to take care of essential needs. When it becomes necessary to leave our homes, we're advised to stay at least six feet away from others and to limit our gatherings with other households.

And so we asked poets... How is your body, your self, your energy responding? Anger, grief, fearful for the future, fearful for the safety of your loved ones, happy to spend time at home or down time with those same loved ones, confused from information overload? How are you responding to self-isolation? How are you responding to others who are responding to self-isolation? What is self-isolation? Are you in the depths of the stages of grief?

This chapbook is a public archive of the accoutrements: a public literary series project of a collaboration between Avenue 50 Studio and Alternative Field and published by Alternative Field Notes. Each published archive is accompanied by a visual art exhibit, a workshop, a community discussion, or a poetry reading. *In Isolation: an anthology* is a literary project in conjunction with Avenue 50 Studio's visual art exhibition responding to art created under the COVID pandemic, Art Under the Influence.

accoutrements: a public literary series is a project made possible with the generous support from:

California Humanities, a non-profit partner of the National Endowment for the Humanities. visit calhum.org

a Local Impact Grant from the California Arts Council. visit arts.ca.gov

This book is dedicated to the ones who miss their loved ones, the ones who have endured and who are enduring, and the ones who are hanging in there.

table of contents

Distancing
Robert Américo Esnard

Learning a mother tongue as a second language requires learning history,
what things are called again, how to rename things, relearning my name
again. I wipe my countertop clean with a disinfecting cloth—a new ritual to
clear any history—and practice Spanish at the spice rack: cumin *comino*,
garlic *ajo*, oregano and cilantro their selves. Sometimes the two tongues

are the same. Yesterday too, I went to the dark cabinet beneath the sink,
unearthed a disposable cloth to clean the same surface. I will do it tomorrow
again. In Spanish I know three ways to articulate the future. The first
the same as English. I will do it *Lo haré*. The second is similar enough,
I am going to do it *Voy a hacerlo,* it simply requires the near future

though there is no standard for what is near. Today I left my apartment
only once, to collect a 90-day supply of insulin—a luxury afforded to me
by my employer so that I can continue to live. It has filled a drawer
in my refrigerator. Again. I didn't even leave for food. In Cuba, I hear,
my family sometimes wants for food. I have all I need, and the news

tells me not to leave. The news plays clips of a debate on socialism,
and I walk the 33 steps from my desk to kitchen to bathroom to bedroom.
My mother calls, and we discuss how my anti-virals to prevent HIV
transmission might help me—despite my risk of infection—even though
they are for my wandering tongue. We will not discuss the last bit again.

Living alone requires becoming your own mother, a second self-preparing
arroz con pollo while the first listens to the news over the home internet radio.
The third articulation of the future in Spanish is indistinguishable
from the present without context. *Lo hago*. This one does not exist
in English. It requires the near future, again, whenever that is. In Cuba,

I hear the doctors are taxi drivers because it is more lucrative. On the news
I hear people are hoarding toilet paper and hand sanitizer, and there
aren't enough hospital beds for everyone. So, I wipe my countertop
clean, and I don't leave my apartment, and I take my insulin and antivirals,
and I cook alone, and I tell my mother I love her. In both English and Spanish

there is a present tense that includes the past. I have done it *Lo he hecho*.
This is distinct from the Spanish future that is otherwise indistinguishable
from the present, which is to say, the past and future are present
in Spanish, but not in English; that the past may be the present or the future
may be the present or simply that the present has a second self in both times.

For a mother tongue to be a second language requires history, requires
cleansing, requires leaving. Yesterday I walked the same 33 steps around my
apartment. Today I hear they have enough anti-virals in Cuba for the world,
despite the taxi drivers. Tomorrow it will not be on the news. Tomorrow
I will not hear a voice besides my own. But I will still practice.

History
Donny Jackson

remember your smile the day before the news crawl was caution tape
the day the sun on the back of your neck was kiss when you laughed all
of your air out of you and no one flinched the day children around your
leg was a wreath remember the day before you started counting days and
know in the locket of your breastbone how that day and smile and sun and
laugh and children like a wreath was exactly like the day before the first
of the first of this nation said thank you for a blanket full of smallpox

Still Life, Origami
Lisa Krueger

Can't breathe, she said. Chest
hurts. To inhale. Isolation flattens
me, she said. My body folds into
itself. Breathe like this, I said, slow
and ocean deep: sound of my
mouth, air from my body, on the
phone. My head is light, she said,
the stars. What if I pass out, I am
all alone. Your breath will bear
you, I said, as a raft. The phone on
my desk went dark, a little black
box; I caught my breath. Twilight,
the whisper of a thousand cranes:
I heard her breathe. I breathed.
Breathing.

How I Spent the End of Days
Daniel Pieczkolon

Mostly doing dishes,
soapy water and singing
Happy birthday to dead celebrities—
sometimes Nina Simone,
sometimes Marilyn Monroe,
but not just women
I would have liked to know.

Practicing gratitude with Kristine,
giving thanks to the artifice
of our jobs, and the real comforts
they afford us, as we estrange
the days from themselves:
Ice cream for breakfast,
sex before lunch,

as the living room blinds
particulate the early afternoon sun,
bend the rays into new shapes
for us to name. I'm as close
to a beard as I've ever been,
and she—brilliant and three days unshowered—
smells more like me than I do.

Scrolling through the news—
people are dying who have never died before—
going for walks and watching
the sky change from periwinkle
to ash to eggplant—
Turns out its false, but
like so many things, it feels true.

Trying our best
to imagine what comes next
and how it could be
as good as we've made this.

Spent
Dorsía Smith Silva

To stand in line on a Tuesday,
while the moon at the coda
of the 4 am edge glistens saffron,
and wait for the food bank
to open at 7 am
is no easy burden.
I breathe in my reality
and place it in my mouth:
the remaining can of tomato sauce
and loaf of white bread
cannot fuse my tightening belly,
and I don't have $10 to
buy eggs.

I rupture by the meat at $19 per pack.
The manager becomes ugly noise: "Still in stock."
My mind pins the clippings of farmers
dumping milk and pushing vegetables
back into the earth.
What it must feel like
to stroke the aperture of new cells
and then pivot to garden skeletons plump
with yearning.
Yes, what I see is a strange arrangement
that has hauled itself
into existence on steady prongs,
in the throes of bottomless theories of the world
that dangle on our ears.

I Wouldn't Settle for Less
Mariah Freire

I.
1 cup desperation
1 ½ cup instant gratification
3 tbs loneliness
8 tbs online shopping addiction (or vice of your choosing)
1 glass wine of the day

In a large bowl sift the desperation to settle your cravings for instant
gratification until fully mixed together. Add loneliness and a pinch of salt
for a drier humor. In a separate bowl combine the wine of the day with
half your vice of choice. Mix until soft and smooth and let sit. Combine
both bowls and wish for something better than disappointment. Bake at
350 degrees forever.

II.
Take the remainder of your wine and pour into as many glasses until
empty. Sip. With the rest of your online shopping addiction and buy a
terrazzo table, monstera deliciosa, millennial pink wrapped in capitalist
comforts, eco-friendly, did you know?

Consider a ceramic one-hitter for the tough days. Consider a new vice.
Consider a new life.

III.
there is nothing as sweet
as the taste of feigned
luxury

who said I can't have
a lick and half a bite? who
said i can't have

overripe, luscious fruit
sticky sweet cinnamon rolls, or
garlicky focaccia until I feel sick

who said I can't have cannabis
flower candles, cashmere loungewear
for breakfast?
lunch?
dinner?

For dessert? Failed delivery

attempt
somewhere bread is broken
and so am I

What Is Left?
Carla Sameth

I.   My rind is being peeled away.
More naked than I've ever been,
but on Zoom, appear fully clothed. Above
the waist. We can strip down below,
where no one can see us. Lie about our scraped
interiors, about our breaking down exterior
that can't be seen because the corridors
of the emergency rooms are filled with people
who can't breathe, and corpses that cannot
leave because there is no space
for more burials. The refrigerated trucks wait
as if delivering perishables. I want to tell them
that I too need cooling down: heart beats too fast,
and I don't know how much longer
this silver linings thing can last

II.   Give me a chance to tell you what
is sweet from that place not seen
on Zoom, if the time hasn't passed. Hope
that I'm not all dry inside, the moisture
sucked out by age and fright. Give me
a chance to show you what I'm made
of: allspice, nutmeg, cinnamon, whatever
is left. Orange rind. Throw it all in there
even if there is nothing to crunch between
teeth, find the softness beneath. Fresh fruit
and vegetables all being picked by those
with nothing: no masks, no gloves,
no social distancing and soon, no job. Here in America,
the food is tossed, the farmers lament, but it costs
too much to harvest and feed those who starve.
Takes too much to keep that 75 -year-old
with a bad kidney alive when the 30 -year-old
who once had a life ahead,
is choking.

III.   At 61, I'm one of the *expendables*;
I get that. After all, I've lived my life,
had my child, loved my loves. But still,
I want to hold that grandchild, caress
my wife, kiss my son. Time doesn't feel
quite up. I hold onto your hand against
the screen. I pray. I laugh. I cry
with you. Words tumble unceremoniously
into your lap off the screen: I love you,
I miss you, I don't want to die without
hugging you one more time.

Chordata: Animals With Backbones
Jasper X

the sky is not yet awake, but the birds are.
they sing to each other from blankets of foliage,
reaching out with their melodic chirps.

it is too dark to see, and yet, they find each other.
newly-born leaves rustle from their elm branches, stirring with
the movement of the wind. the birds sing to each other,
but their song doesn't go unheard from the rest of the world.
their notes carry.

and the notes reach the trunk of the trees, winding down to the
very core of a collection of rings. and the notes reach
a hollow space between steel and glass,
reverberating and becoming more complex than
they were before. and the notes reach the ears of a teenager
settled in 4AM's skin, who is too familiar with the feeling of being
one of the only things awake. and the notes reach.
and the notes reach.

the birds are so used to this isolation, the quietness of
being what feels like the only source of life, so
they do not fear humming out into the void. they do not fear making
their presence known to the world around them.
they do not fear company, which is why they sing to the
birds around them. which is why they let their
song reach out. which is why they remain awake throughout the day.
which is why the song continues.

and the sky, it will awaken. and the cars, they will start up.
and the people, they will speak. and the teenager dressed in
the flesh of 4AM, they will hold the not-so secret song of the birds
close to their chest and it will become their song…
silently hummed at first, a loop on the brain, before it morphs
and articulates itself into words and phrases and sentences
and verses. it is not a crime to be known.

the notes, they carry. the song must go on.

Threshold
Amy Dupcak

I lengthen my step
across the unknown
where callery pear trees

bloom like brides
for no one. where sunlight slips
between shadows & ghosts.

where church bells stir
a distant memory and the air
sweeps debris along empty streets.

where every breath is a rebellion.
where nothing becomes something
in the absence of everything

and the earth still turns
without mourning or fear,
loyal only to herself.

People Watching Indoors
Nesima Aberra

Mom rotates between three spots in the house
Kitchen
        laundry room
                living room floor
The black reading glasses sit on her nose more now
She uses a faded folded paper
As a bookmark for her Quran
Reaches for the blue, red and green glossy prayer beads
The way I reach for my phone

She sneaks away to have a muffled conversation
with a relative overseas
Clicking her tongue
I have memorized the words she repeats
In each call I grow frustrated
by how the virus is stealing
lives and our time

Dad sits in the weathered seat of his swivel chair
Squinting at two monitors
in the dark in his bedroom
folders and papers are scattered around his desk
His commute has become between there and his bed

He insists on having warm, not cold water, with
two slices of lemon
The water once was sitting in a clay pot
"Because it gives it life"
I smell the ginger candies on his breath

Later, Mom brings him a spoonful of black seed oil
Because someone sent something on whatsapp that claimed
It could protect us against the virus
As I stand in the hallway, he asks why
Am I not drinking black seed oil too

Do I drink it for his sake or mine

Le Karnice
Vanessa Bernice De La Cruz

This is healing.
This is inside the cocoon.
This is waiting for the sun to rise
This is covering ourselves in fabric
Waiting for the wounds to stop festering
And lay flat.
Knowing they might not
Knowing they may remain tiny hills
Today and tomorrow and the month after that

It is being buried alive
And looking for a bell to ring
To signal you are looking for a way out
But not finding it
It is getting your hands dirty
And breathing in mud

It is six feet under
And six feet apart.

The One of What I've Learned
Brittany Mosley

1. I know how to chart the angles
of the sun through my window
with each passing hour:
the leaning shadows across my carpet,
the minute it bathes my desk,
the moment when each memory
along the shelf will be warm to the touch,
full of life as it hasn't been in years.
I understand, now,
the great triumph it was
for the ancients to chart the stars.

2. I should no longer reject clichés.
We are not promised tomorrow.
I know this now.

3. The precision of a paintbrush
does not matter when working
with watercolors.
The paint goes where it wants,
its own conception of correctness.
The shades always look even
until the water dries
and the harsh lines return.
Somehow, it looks better like that.

4. Fear dissolves with time.
In the beginning I'd go downstairs
and check to make sure
the door was bolted and chained
and then I'd go back up to sleep
and then I'd go back down and check
and then I'd go back up to sleep
and then I'd go back down to check
and then

.

Now, I look once before flicking off the light.
And I am okay.

5. You do not start a puzzle
by assembling the main image.
You start with the very edges,
the ridged fringes that are
easiest to distinguish not by their color,
but their shape.
And then you find where everything goes
in the background. The soft parts,
the parts that are somehow not in focus.
A focal point is not always
what is most important.

6. I have not learned,
but I am learning
to be okay with myself.
With my knotted thoughts and
the works of my hands and
the past I've painted with too many colors
until it was mud-brown.
I was never meant
to pull the sun below the horizon
and tell the world it is night.
I am worth something no matter how small
my ripples in eternity will be.

*the poem first appeared as part of
Retelling of Now in *Pleaseseeme.com*

The Washing and the Wringing
Xochitl-Julisa Bermejo

The yellow-eyed cat saunters from room to room.
Her poison-soaked paw prints spell out CANCELLED
across the floor, and we play lava trying not to touch.

By day, an invisible sick spreads over the surfaces
of shopping carts, crosswalk buttons, brown packages
on front steps, and we scrub hands trying not to touch.

I lose paying gigs, Bumble dates, possibility, but savor
tiny morsels of time like sautéing onions and 5pm dinner
with the parents while our hands do their best not to touch.

At night, glasses of red wine and conversations on loop
soothe or don't. I pad to bed, forget la Llorona and her
insatiable need, bring hands below blankets, enjoy touch.

Solitary Confinement
Cassondra Windwalker

I am building a folly on the edge
of the sea: walls of quartz and coal,
steps of driftwood, windows framed
with fishbones and chiton shells,
sea-gusts for mortar and a roof of clouds:

I will climb my tower and look
for you over the mountains – I hope
you are building a folly, too,
hope your hands are dusty and calloused,
your eyes crusted with sand
and your feet bare on the cliffside path:

send up a signal
in the smoke of the cathedrals
and I will say your name aloud
in my empty halls,
I will trace in bruises
the echo of your voice on my chest.

Pandemic Ode: A Partial Prayer
MJ

after Airea D. Matthews

Praise be to solitude silence.
Praise be to steam's ascent through grate's clenched teeth, to
outstretched knees that hop over.
Praise be to corner store bodegas stocking single roll toilet paper.
Praise be to pure lungs.
Praise be to love & its discovery under overturned & broken stone.
Praise the butterfly wings &
    whistled winds which carry them. Praise be to my son's curl pattern
    & nap [3 hours down].
Praise be to the loctician-turned-therapist
disintegrating worry with strong hands at scalp; praise be to the scalp & kitchen
the thick of it pulled in lover's grip.
    Praise be to sidewalk graffiti sprawl: LOVE IS MONEY.
Praise be to fixed mortgages & rent control.
Praise be to bob & weave wheelie poppin scraper bikes blessing Lake Merritt
with bronze & tin sunrays.
Praise the 5 paper white pelicans in synchronized syncopated swim;
    Amen to their squad goals.
Praise be to the 18 bus &
to Green Naked Ladies' blurring route's landscape.

Praise be to the awning –
    its voluptuous curvature;
Praise the teeth grazing teat, scrape scream & shout Lord's name in vain,
Praise the tight tunnel collapse around fingers.
Praise be to the sideshow
    & skid marks tires burn & singe;
    Praise be to Oakland's breathing ghosts. Praise be to
Sinaloa; to the white Goldilocked creature standing barefoot
in its parking lot; praise the shit talk & cut up within earshot.
Praise be to poets who know it & poets who don't.
Praise be to ugly ducklings who stay that way.
Praise be to threaded brows; fluorescent hair; sundresses & golden wing ear cuffs.

Praise be to guitars & bodies
        after their shape, supple for strum.
Praise be to skunk
seeping outta every low parked car on this block.
Praise be to the tents sandbagging the city streets;
to stakes that hold them down; to the masked
unwavering handing out hygiene & nutrition.

Praise be to black trans praise dancers; to electrified
prayer hands.
Praise the cities of refuge.
Praise this sea of black & brown worshippers whirring still air into sandstorm.
Praise be to the uncontrolled organist; to peach cobbler;
        to jumpin shoutin cryin. Praise be to the shimmering wave of fans
        preparing for flight.
Praise be to unnamed spirit. Praise be to
        altar; to those not here; to the exiled.
Praise the leaps & weeps of faith; the rocking in arms' cradle & holler.
Praise be to tilled soil;
        to grape vines; to jasmine. Praise be to indigoes & violets;
        to the color purple.
Praise be to our skin & its basement organs; to belly's wax & wane.
Praise be to the elemental.
Praise the body & its stardust; the tear's cleansing saltwater.
Praise be to remembrance &
        to release when memory grows anvil.
Praise be to Harvest moon bathwaters; to balm of a mother's sweet song.
Praise be to incantation, to utterance.
Praise be to the elemental.
Praise be to diaspora; to
        calloused hands & hearts thumping on in defiance.
Praise be to defiance. Praise be to hummingbird's flight.

In the Quiet
Melora Walters

The refrigerator coughs cold
chunks of gray and white,

clumps of cat hair
in the blanket, soft
like the naked foot that
slips into the water to
check the temperature,
the sound it leaves is a
padded secret dollop of
silk pudding on broken
china,

the two halves placed neatly
side by side in the cabinet, like
the two large ears of Anubis his
face turned slightly to the left
with his Mona Lisa smile.

Two fossilized bones of the inner
ear of an ancient whale flank the
shape of the heart.

Two large wings flap
and flap and flap to
find the air.

Instructions for a Modern Pandemic
Noriko Nakada

Read the news	Never read the news
Stock up on essentials	You won't know what is essential until the shelves empty
Wash your hands	Count and sing
Take deep breaths	If you cannot take a deep breath, worry
Meditate and think of nothing	Don't meditate if it makes you think of everything
Eat all of the things	Eat nothing
Drink to make yourself bigger	Drink to make the world smaller
In the morning, forget	Don't forget that you are made of water
Get outside	Stay home
Connect with people	Stay alone
Locate intimacy	Remain isolated
Count the days	Lose track of time
Let the hours, days; weeks melt away	Melt away
Pay attention to bees and moths	Smash the bugs
Watch the sun and moon rise and fall	Never look at the sun
Don't lose yourself	Lose yourself

During My Daily Phone Call To Her Assisted Living Facility, My
Mother Explains That She Is Slowly Fading Away...

Marjorie Maddox

And it is not the light but the dust in the light
that rises, plunges, plateaus on the short *hhhhh*
of my exhale, less final than a sigh that dies
from hopelessness but, still there,
heavy, scattered. Near dusk and it peppers
voice in the *Oh* of the weighty unseen,
voice unraveling the feared,
the obvious.

And it is not
the distance between words,
between parent/child, not the desert under the plane,
or the plane cruising above and past the jagged mountains,
the wholesome prairies, the vast expanse of flat nothing
I've come to expect from questions,
those dust-to-dust queries that filter,
block, blind, restrict, restrain. Not the miles

but those same damn particles that rise, plunge,
plateau on the long *hhhhhhhhh* of my exhale;
that now wrap the plane, the air, the distance,
not in dust, but this inhale of what could or could not be
transmitted from the state of my loved ones here—in the fear
where we cower together—two thousand miles cross country
to her, love on lockdown, vulnerability
the only transportation

and the law
and what we can and cannot speak.
All the while my mother and I stay
where we are: the dust still swirls;
she still breathes on the other end of the line.
"I am slowly fading away," she states again,
matter-of-factly, voice so slight
it unravels me.

Nowhere to go but here,
daily rerun of routine. Ear to a phone,
listening. Dust-in-light rising.
Exhale/inhale a life, *hhhhhhhhhhhhhhhh*
multiplied. Or halved. "I am
slowly fading away," I state again,
matter-of-factly, my voice so slight
it unravels her.

Quarantine, day 27: The Dishes
Adrienne Pilon

Always the washing up.
The coffee mugs, the buttered knives
Dishes multiplying like ants or
wasps at spring's start, the way termites
emerge with the warm, climbing out
windowsills by the dozens.

The dishwasher runs overtime.
By lunch there's another load
to unload. Plate stacks grow like
weeds after a warm rain in May.
The crumbed plates, the crusted spoons.
Sponges tire out, fibers going flat.
Rubber gloves turn to glue.
When did we ever cook so much?
Where did this pie server come from?

By evening dishes have multiplied
like rabbits in June.
The knife between the couch cushions
may have hosted a brie.
A cocktail glass on the landing,
its bottom a scrim of brown.
A cereal bowl in the entryway
cemented with cocoa puffs.
The long-lost spatula appears
behind the dryer, coated with dust.

We stand at the sink all day
soap on our hands, soaked to the waist
looking out the window into the yard
where dirty plates and glasses are strewn,
scattered, like wildflowers in a field we
walked through last year, or the year before.
Wasps buzz and swirl around the dishes
vying for the leavings in
a springtime ecstasy.

Kendra Preston Leonard

I
singing at home
alone
to the dog
to the peonies—
soft pink face-surrounding cloud touching whole-engulfing—
I saw
in
someone else's camera

II
how cherished curbs are now:
they are the site of interaction excitement transfer

the places where food and medicines
and books
sit
in focus
on the edge of concrete
plump with fulfillment

becoming damp
in the humidity

the gently sweating singer at the party—
on the stage, waiting for you to come closer
listen

III
strum and pick—
fingers on a pillow—

light, light
longer

haven't you written some songs by now?
baked all the breads of the world?
braided them all into a challah of sound?

the kitchen is empty and dark

Matthew Andrews

1.

The instructions are as old
and as thick
as the branches of apple trees:

Purify thyself.

Good doors
make
good lovers.

A little yeast
leavens the whole batch.

One sip and you are drunk,
the moisture of your mouth
giving life to spores and weeds,

spreading its seed.

2.

Even after generations of exposure
there is still so much we do not understand.

Is it the ache of an empty plaza,
the congregation of aborted memories,
the rush of anonymous skin brushing against?

Is if the concrete barriers of quarantine,
just the two of us, sharing form,
exchanging familiar parasites for new ones?

Or is it the war drum rhythm of heartbeat,
the wheezing of exertion, the growing fire
from inside that burns away flesh?

3.

You and me, we are
a knotted mass of yarn

in a drawer, a messy orgy
of molecules with wildly tangled limbs.

I empty into you like a river
and then take from you like a cloud,

and you do the same, symbiotes
in a revolving door of breath,

bedmates with open eyes,
mutual destruction assured.

4.

Outside a closed window, history: sagas
written in starlight, each pulsating
with endless strands of time,
the sentences all stacked atop one another
as in the diary of a madman,

the way wrinkles collect
in the corners of closed eyes,

the way organisms dance
wildly in a petri dish.

April 16, 2020
Richard Henkle

Someone used
The word
Halcyon
Today, but I
Didn't know
Its meaning.

Google tells me it is
Pleasant memories
Of ages past.

Who knew *halcyon* could include
Just a month ago--

When I high-fived Kevin, and promised Tara I'd join her next pub crawl;
When I blocked out a week in April to take the 10th grade class to visit
colleges in New York;
When I put off getting my hair cut because Amber didn't have any time in
her schedule that
       wouldn't overlap with my plans for happy hours, staff meetings,
       or my night to make dinner;
When teaching meant standing in front of a classroom, watching students
       grasp a metaphor in a poem for the first time;
When I bought a plane ticket to see my cousin get married in California;
When I watched college basketball on television, as the game was
happening;
When commercial breaks were about selling products rather than
       reminding people to practice social distancing;
When I wasn't yet familiar with the term *social distancing*;
When I went to church on Sunday morning, and Cub Scouts on Tuesday night;
When Thursday evenings had soccer practice;
When, short of asafoetida powder or Tupelo honey, any ingredient I
       wanted for dinner was available at the grocery store;
When my neighbor could see me smile at him if we passed on a walk;

When I didn't realize just how halcyonic life was.

Flower
Kathleen Klassen

I write myself out of this purpling
winter, black
and blue toes, covid
snows in May.

I write myself out of these night-blusters
cold wraps, icy surfaces
stainless steel and plastic
lingers for days they say.

I write myself out of these sleepless inhales
stifled exhales
viral floret
dances on a breath.

I write myself out of this gripping
trapped-inside
four-walled
skull-cage.

And it's still winter
though the lilac
still winter
though the violet
still winter
though the iris
still winter
until fields of lavender.

Then purple will find its flower
and write me back
into bloom.

Not the End of Poetry
Lana Hechtman Ayers

after Ada Limón

Shower me with susurrus and hummingbird,
with cherry blossoms and Steller's Jay,
with acorn and pine needle, leaves and roots,
more impasto, more of still and perhaps,
more witty librarian and awake and a moment's
grace, more of flesh and ache, desire and divine
remembering, and the heavens and ice floes,
sorrow, more of everything the pain is like and not
like, how someone's absence changes the light,
more of the pledges and denials and studying
the sky and searching one's heart, more of the flare,
the flash, a best friend's death and the letter stuffed
in a shoebox, more of the hunger and craving,
the self-doubt and all of suffering, more of lost
childhoods, grandmothers and grandfathers, more
considering the world, curious and passionate, more
of the difficult to look at without looking away, more
please listen I am here, more we are in this together,
more of your voice mingling with mine, more nights,
stars, moons, gratitude and its gifts, more joy,
I am asking you to write more poems.

Sensing
Janet Powers

Before you begin to hurt
or cough or breathe too hard,
they say you lose your sense
of taste and also smell.
Each day I check on small
things: ginseng in the tea,
lime tortilla chips, peas
in butter sauce, sensations
of life, tasting and smelling,
wouldn't want to lose either one,
even for a short while.

While we play the waiting game,
I'm not eating the usual things.
Chalk it up to coupons or
drawing down a loaded larder,
rewarding self with foods
coveted but not allowed
by the diet police – one way
to cope with confinement:
dependent for pleasure
on tasting and smelling,
hoping they won't go away.

What I've Learned in A Pandemic
Jayne Moore Waldrop

I've learned to really wash my hands,
not half-assed attempts but deep cleaning
each crevasse, bumpy knuckle, age spot.
I've learned to scrub like it will save me.

I've learned not to touch my face or nose,
hug a friend, lean in to hear a whisper,
take someone's hand, fist bump a kid.
I've learned to keep my distance.

I've learned to mix a 1:100 bleach ratio
for relentless wipe downs, still wishing
I could pass the job to someone else.
I've learned cleaning is an act of love.

I've learned I favor the same old jeans
from an overstuffed closet, stocked
for another time, another way of life.
I've learned I intend to travel lighter.

I've learned humans can go unwaxed,
unpainted, undyed, and untrimmed,
but hair still needs to be washed.
I've learned to sip tea while I bathe.

I've learned to make do, not make
another trip, accept substitutions,
unfamiliar brands, bruised apples.
I've learned things aren't worth the fuss.

I've learned that spring keeps coming.
I miss the woods, but around me I see
trees bud, flowers bloom, birds mate.
I've learned squirrels are urgent nesters.

I've learned to Zoom for family visits,
go to church on Facebook Live,
chat over drinks staring into a screen.
I've learned introverts get lonely, too.

I've learned that snarky posts become
final testaments chiseled into virtual
stone with no chance to edit or delete.
I've learned to reconsider my legacy.

I've learned to hunt and gather online,
how to make masks, relearned how
to thread a sewing machine bobbin.
I've learned to resuscitate old skills.

I've learned the coronavirus isn't picky.
It finds us – rich, poor, urban, rural –
but it's not colorblind when it attacks.
I learned it may be American after all.

I've learned about flattened curves,
that being 60+ years makes us targets,
my beloved older siblings even more so.
I've learned life moves unbelievably fast.

I've learned the precious mechanics
of breathing, how ventilators work,
that patients panic like they're drowning.
I've learned rescuers keep them sedated.

I've learned seemingly healthy folks
may be carriers, whether it's a novel virus,
a hateful spirit, a contagious disregard.
I've learned few are immune from fear.

I've learned, as I wait, to look deeper,
examine my own sore spots, hurt places
I'd long hoped had healed but haven't.
I've learned love may be the oldest cure.

April
Yusra Amjad

April is the cruellest month.
All regrowth. Breeding lilacs out of dead land.
All recovery. Mixing memory and desire.
All reconciliation. Stirring dull roots with spring rain.
My whole life, an April.
Forever finding out
I still haven't died.
Forever wrenching
myself back to life.
Forever pushing grass blades
through unyielding earth.
Forever unfurling new buds
against all odds.
Slow.
Painstaking.
Inevitable.

Healing is
the cruellest process.
Hope is
the cruellest thing.
I am
perpetual spring,
and oh god,
it hurts.

On Hubble Telescope's Thirtieth Birthday

Emily Hockaday

Just when I'm really feeling sorry
for myself, and my home, for all of our planet,
for my mom, and my daughter who isn't yet three
and doesn't understand why she can't go to daycare,
(then again for myself), my spouse, for my city,
for the way the sirens echo down Woodhaven,
a photograph is released

of the Magellanic Cloud
from Hubble Telescope. Inside a red nebula,
masses of stars ten times the size of our sun
are forming—gestational winds snake plasma
into bubbles where stars will be born. Our sun
is small, middle aged, modestly decorated
with planets. We are incomprehensibly
unimportant. Maybe I needed to remember;
the pressure doesn't have to feel
so great. The stakes, even
for our very lives,
aren't high.

Bios

Nesima Aberra (she/her) is a writer, poet, and digital strategist, based in Virginia. She is the daughter of Eritrean immigrants. Nesima is passionate about working at the intersection of storytelling and social good. Learn more about her work at nesimaaberra.com.

Yusra Amjad is a poet and comedian from Lahore, Pakistan. She is a graduate of Forman Christian College and a Fulbright scholar pursuing her MFA at Sarah Lawrence. She has been published by *The Missing Slate, Crossed Genres, Cities+Secrets,* Where Are You Press, Rising Phoenix Press, and *The Noble Gas Quarterly,* and was an honourable mention for the 2016 Judith Khan Memorial Prize and a finalist for the inaugural Zeenat Haroon Prize. She was also nominated for the 2016 Pushcart Prize by *The Missing Slate* under a pseudonym for her poem 'Muhammad'. Her work has appeared in the *Mongrel Book of Voices* and the *Aleph Review.*

Based in Modesto, California, **Matthew Andrews** is a full-time private investigator and part-time journalist, writer, and poet. His poetry has appeared or is forthcoming in *pacificREVIEW, Deep Wild Journal, Song of the San Joaquin*, and *Eunonia Review*, among others.

Lana Hechtman Ayers, night-owl, coffee-enthusiast, has authored nine poetry collections and a time travel novel. She lives on the Oregon coast where she enjoys the near-constant plunk of rain on the roof and the sea's steady whoosh. Lana leads writing workshops in Tillamook, a town with more cows than humans. Visit her online at LanaAyers.com.

Xochitl-Julisa Bermejo is the daughter of Mexican immigrants and the author of *Posada: Offerings of Witness and Refuge* (Sundress Publications 2016). A former Steinbeck Fellow, Poets & Writers California Writers Exchange winner, and Barbara Deming Memorial Fund grantee, she's received residencies from Hedgebrook, Ragdale, National Parks Arts Foundation, and Poetry Foundation. She has work published in *Acentos Review, CALYX, crazyhorse*, and *American Poetry Review* among others. A dramatization of her poem "Our Lady of the Water Gallons," directed by Jesús Salvador Treviño, can be viewed at latinopia.com. She is a member of Miresa Collective and director of Women Who Submit. xochitljulisa.wordpress.com

Vanessa Bernice De La Cruz is a self-taught artist and writer from Los Angeles, CA. She has been scribbling and doodling for as long as she can remember but has only recently decided to share those things and infuse them with sense. You can find her hanging out with her cat, whining on social media @alienraynedrop, or you can visit her not fully constructed website vbdelacruz.com

Amy Dupcak is writer, teacher, and editor living in Manhattan. Her short story collection, *Dust,* was published on Lucid River Press, and her work has appeared in *Sonora Review, Hypertext, Phoebe, Fringe, Litro, District Lit,* and other journals. She earned her MFA in Fiction from The New School, acts as an assistant editor of *Cagibi* journal, and writes themed trivia for the long-running literary and performance series Lyrics, Lit & Liquor.

Robert Américo Esnard was born and raised in the Bronx, NY. He studied Linguistics and Cognitive Science at Dartmouth College. His work has been published by *Glass, Alternating Current Press / The Coil, Lunch Ticket,* and several anthologies. He is a Best of the Net and Pushcart Prize-nominated poet.

Mariah Freire is a New York born and raised poet. She holds a degree in Communications from Boston University and lives in Brooklyn with two cats. She is an Aquarius.

After more than ten years on Capitol Hill, **Richard Henkle** decided that if he was going to spend his days with people who acted like teenagers, they should be teenagers. So he now teaches humanities classes at a private school in Reston, Virginia. He holds an MA in Literature and Humanities from Marymount University, and has work forthcoming in *Inkblot.* He lives in Herndon, Virginia with his wife and two children.

Emily Hockaday's newest chapbook, *Beach Vocabulary,* is forthcoming from Red Bird Chaps. She is author of *Space on Earth, Ophelia: A Botanist's Guide, What We Love & Will Not Give Up,* and *Starting a Life.* Her poems have appeared in journals including *Newtown Literary, The Maine Review,* and *Salt Hill.* She is Managing Editor of *Analog Science Fiction & Fact* and *Asimov's Science Fiction,* and can be found on web at www. emilyhockaday.com and @E_Hockaday.

MJ is a Black, queer non-binary poet & parent living in Oakland, CA. Their work is featured or forthcoming at *Kissing Dynamite, Rigorous Mag, & Borderlands Texas Poetry Review.* They are an Assistant Poetry Editor at *Foglifter Press.* MJ has received fellowships from the Hurston/Wright Foundation, SF Writers Grotto, VONA, & Kearny Street Workshop. They are currently the Community Engagement Graduate Fellow in the MFA program at Mills College.

Donny Jackson is a poet, doctor of clinical psychology, and an Emmy-winning producer of documentary television based in Los Angeles. His debut volume of poetry, *boy,* was published by Silver Star Laboratory in February 2020. donnyjacksonpoetry.com/boy

Kathleen Klassen was an Ottawa high school teacher for over 20 years. A new writer who discovered poetry as a source of healing after an injury, she has been published on *Bywords.ca, passagerbooks.com,* with *In/Words Magazine* and Press and looks forward to an upcoming publication with ottawater.

Lisa C. Krueger's poetry has appeared in various journals, including *Ploughshares, Alaska Quarterly Review, Prairie Schooner,* and *About Place*; Red Hen Press has published collections of their poems. They are a psychologist in Los Angeles.

Kendra Preston Leonard is a poet, lyricist, and librettist whose work is inspired by the local, historical, and mythopoeic. Her first chapbook, *Making Mythology*, was published in 2020 from Louisiana Literature Press, and her work appears in numerous publications including *vox poetica, The Waggle,* and *Lily Poetry Review*. Leonard collaborates regularly with composers on works including new operas and song cycles. Follow her on Twitter at @K_Leonard_PhD or visit her site at https://kendraprestonleonard.hcommons.org/.

Professor of English and Creative Writing at Lock Haven University, **Marjorie Maddox** has published 11 collections of poetry—including *Transplant, Transport, Transubstantiation* (Yellowglen Prize); *True, False, None of the Above* (Illumination Book Award Medalist); *Local News from Someplace Else; Perpendicular As I* (Sandstone Book Award)—the prose collection *What She Was Saying* (Fomite); 4 children's books; *Common Wealth: Contemporary Poets on Pennsylvania* (co-editor); *Presence* (assistant editor); and 600+ stories, essays, and poems in journals and anthologies. www.marjoriemaddox.com

Brittany Mosley is a recent graduate of The Ohio State University with a degree in English. She worked as a reader for *The Journal* and a blogger for Ohio State's undergraduate blog, and is a freelance writer and journalist. Her work has appeared in *Curieux Academic Journal*, but this would be her first publication of poetry.

Noriko Nakada writes, blogs, tweets, parents, and teaches middle school in Los Angeles. She is committed to writing thought-provoking creative non-fiction, fiction, and poetry. Publications include the *Through Eyes Like Mine* memoir series. Excerpts, essays, and poetry have been published in *Kartika, Catapult, Meridian, Compose, Hippocampus,* and *Linden Avenue*.

Daniel Pieczkolon lives in Philadelphia and teaches in the English Department at Arcadia University. His poetry has recently appeared in *Crack the Spine, Rust + Moth,* and *Kettle Blue Review*. He was a 2018 Best of the Net nominee, and he is the editor of the print-only arts zine *Deviant Philly*.

Adrienne Pilon is a teacher and writer. Some of her recent work can be found in *Blanket Sea Journal, Oddball Magazine,* and *BoomerLitMag*. A native Californian, she lives in North Carolina with her family.

"Professor Emerita at Gettysburg College, I taught South Asian literature and civilization, women's studies and peace studies for 49 years. I've published in many small journals, including *Azure, Chaleur, Earth's Daughters, The Poeming Pigeon* and *The Gyroscope Review*. My chapbook, *Difficult to Subdue as the Wind*, appeared in 2009. This old lady still writes poetry despite, or because of, our sorry world." - **Janet Powers**

Carla Sameth's memoir, *One Day on the Gold Line*, was published July 2019. Her work on blended/unblended, queer, biracial and single parenting appears in a variety of literary journals and anthologies. A Pasadena Rose Poet, a Pride Poet with West Hollywood, and a former PEN in The Community Teaching Artist, Carla teaches creative writing to high school and university students, and to incarcerated youth. She has an MFA from Queens University of Charlotte (LatinAm). https://carlasameth.com/

Dorsía Smith Silva is a Professor at the University of Puerto Rico. Her poetry has been published in several journals and magazines in the United States, Canada, and the Caribbean, including *Portland Review, Mom Egg Review, Stoneboat, Atlantis: Critical Studies in Gender, Culture & Social Justice, Moko Magazine*, and elsewhere. She is also the editor of *Latina/Chicana Mothering* and the co-editor of six books. She is currently mastering the art of making rosemary bread.

Jayne Moore Waldrop is the author of *RETRACING MY STEPS*, a finalist in the New Women's Voices Poetry Chapbook Contest (Finishing Line Press 2019). Her work has appeared in *Appalachian Heritage, Still: The Journal, New Limestone Review, Anthology of Appalachian Writers, Deep South Magazine*, and other journals. She lives in Lexington, Kentucky.

Melora Walters is an artist, poet, film maker, and actress. Her poems have been published by Finishing Line Press, Writ Large Press, Serpentine Press, *DRYLAND Lit*, and *Levure Littéraire*. In 2016 she wrote and directed her short film "The Muse", 2017 her first feature "Waterlily Jaguar", and in 2019 "Drowning," which premiered at The Rome Film Festival. Her art has been exhibited in New York, Los Angeles, and Berlin. She has two children, Tom and Joanna.

Cassondra Windwalker is a poet, essayist, and novelist presently residing on the southern coast of Alaska. She welcomes conversations with readers through social media. www.twitter.com/WindwalkerWrite / www.instagram.com/CassondraWindwalker / www.facebook.com/CassondraWindwalkerWrites

Jasper X is a tragedy in the making. They're a Muslim, nonbinary, and queer poet based in Chicago, but what makes them tragic is the fact that they are suspended in that awkward time between childhood and adulthood. When they aren't lamenting over being a sophomore in high school, they're either writing, reading, studying bones, or watching *Bon Appetit*. Find them on @jx.mark on Instagram or in pacificREVIEW's 2020 "*synchronous*" under the name Safa Abdullah.

www.ingramcontent.com/pod-product-compliance
Lightning Source LLC
Chambersburg PA
CBHW030756110726
47900CB00008B/2630